5
5
9
9

13
13
cresc.

MID-INTERMEDIATE

# Ave Maria

TWO PIANOS, FOUR HANDS

Includes duplicate insert

Bach - Gounod

Arr. by Lucile Hinman

THE WILLIS MUSIC COMPANY

# Ave Maria

For Two Pianos-Four hands

BACH-GOUNOD
Arr. by Lucile Hinman

PIANO I

PIANO II

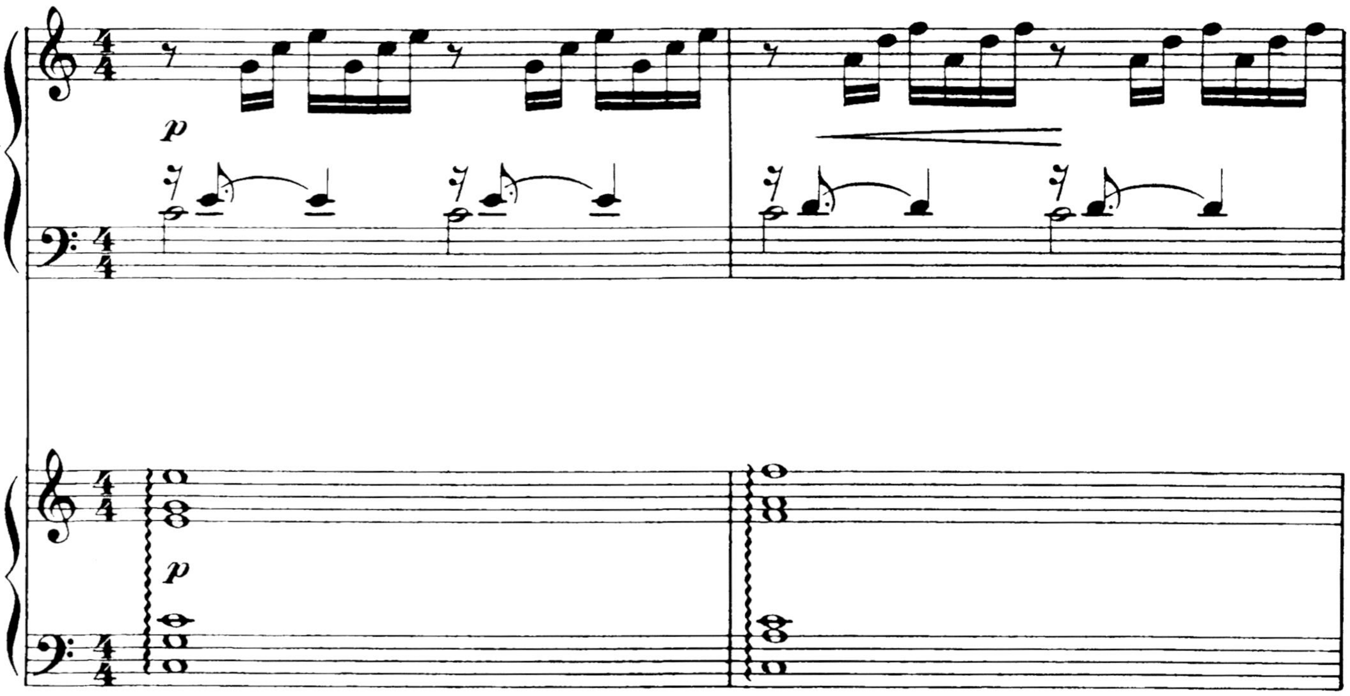

Notice the Pedal Point Bass

The Accompanying 2nd part must be played with organ-like breadth of tone. Piano I is Prelude No. 1 from the well-tempered Clavichord.

17
17
dim.
21
21
cresc.

25
25

MID-INTERMEDIATE

# Ave Maria

TWO PIANOS, FOUR HANDS

PIANO II

**Bach - Gounod**

*Arr. by Lucile Hinman*

THE WILLIS MUSIC COMPANY

# Ave Maria

For Two Pianos-Four hands

BACH-GOUNOD
Arr. by Lucile Hinman

Notice the Pedal Point Bass

The Accompanying 2nd part must be played with organ-like breadth of tone. Piano I is Prelude No. 1 from the well-tempered Clavichord.

5
9

13
13
cresc.

17
17
dim.
21
21
cresc.

25
25

29
29
rit.
33 p
rit.
p 33

29
29
rit.
rit.
33 p
p 33

# More Duets and Ensembles from Willis Music

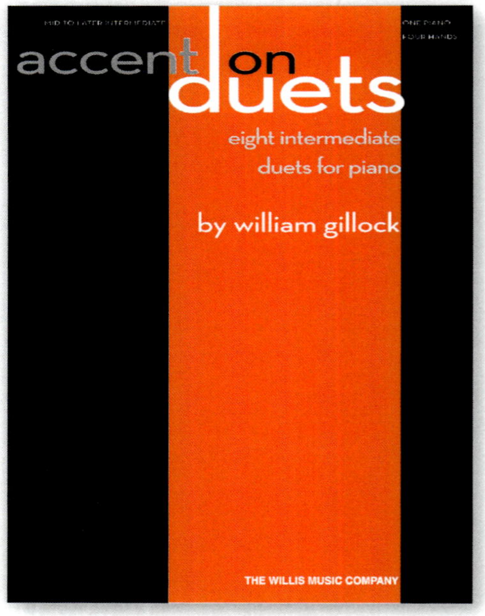


**ACCENT ON DUETS**
Mid to Later Intermediate 00416804

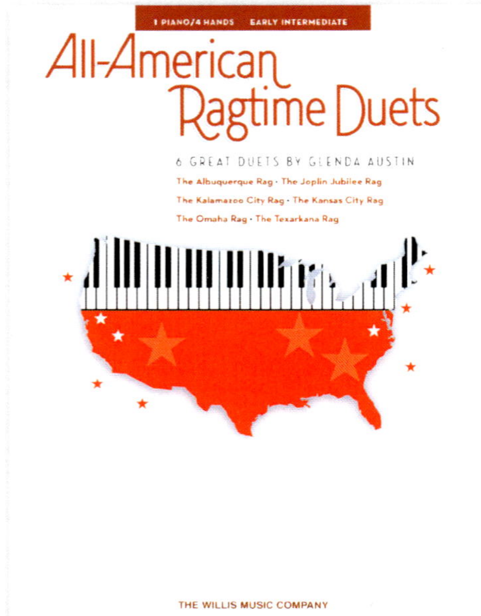


**ALL-AMERICAN RAGTIME DUETS**
Early Intermediate 00416822

**CHAMPAGNE TOCCATA**
Early Advanced 00404388

**ACCENT ON TWO PIANOS**
Intermediate to Advanced 00146176

**NEW ORLEANS JAZZ STYLES DUETS**
Early Intermediate 00416805

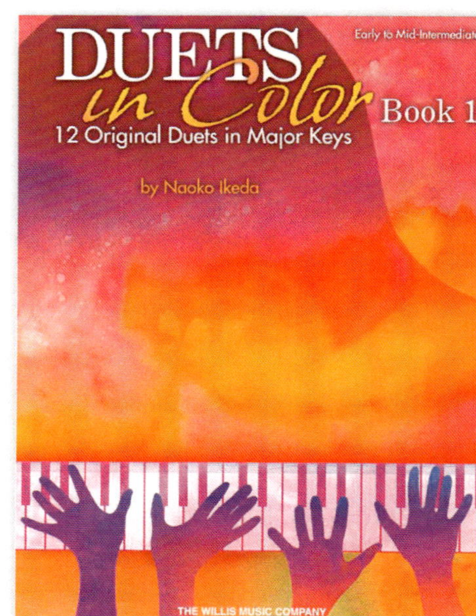


**DUETS IN COLOR – Book 1**
Early to Mid-Intermediate 00416898

ISBN-13: 978-1-5400-3979-8

Distributed By
HAL LEONARD

00411831 9 781540 039798

HL00411831

0 73999 75813 9

WILLIS MUSIC

EXCLUSIVELY DISTRIBUTED BY
HAL•LEONARD®
7777 W. BLUEMOUND RD. P.O. BOX 13819
MILWAUKEE, WISCONSIN 53213

Visit Hal Leonard Online at
**www.halleonard.com**

U.S. $4.99